Christian Character Development SERIES

Who Am I to God?

Group
Loveland, Colorado

Group's R.E.A.L. Guarantee to you:

This Group resource incorporates our R.E.A.L. approach to ministry—one that encourages long-term retention and life transformation. It's ministry that's:

Relational
Because learner-to-learner interaction enhances learning and builds Christian friendships.

Experiential
Because what learners experience through discussion and action sticks with them up to 9 times longer than what they simply hear or read.

Applicable
Because the aim of Christian education is to equip learners to be both hearers and doers of God's Word.

Learner-based
Because learners understand and retain more when the learning process takes into consideration how they learn best.

Note:
The price of this text includes the right for you to make as many copies of the studies as you need for your immediate church group. If another church or organization wants copies of these studies, it must purchase *Christian Character Development Series: Who Am I to God?* for its own use.

Christian Character Development Series: Who Am I to God?

2002 edition

Visit our Web site: **www.grouppublishing.com**

Credits

Contributing Authors: Nancy Going, Siv M. Ricketts, and Jane Vogel

Editor: Debbie Gowensmith

Creative Development Editor: Karl Leuthauser

Chief Creative Officer: Joani Schultz

Copy Editor: Betty Taylor

Art Director: Randy Kady

Cover Art Director: Jeff A. Storm

Computer Graphic Artist: Pat Miller

Cover Design: Alan Furst, Inc. Art and Design

Illustrator: Amy Bryant

Production Manager: Peggy Naylor

ISBN 0-7644-2429-7

10 9 8 7 6 5 4 3 2 1 11 10 09 08 07 06 05 04 03 02

Printed in Canada.

Contents

Introduction

Our teenagers may be talking the talk, but are they walking the walk? Often an enormous gap exists between the Christian values many teenagers claim to have and their actions. Take a moment to ponder these sobering statistics:

• Six out of ten Christian teens say there is no such thing as absolute truth.

• One out of four deny the notion that acting in disobedience to God's laws brings about negative consequences.

• One-half believe the main purpose of life is enjoyment and personal fulfillment.

• Almost half contend that sometimes lying is necessary.

What's wrong with this picture?

Today's teenagers face more choices than any teenagers before them have. They are asked to interpret, evaluate, and make moral decisions within a culture that ignores morality and changes rapidly. The choices your teenagers make today have eternal consequences. Can their faith keep up?

How can we help? We can begin by taking them on a journey—a journey toward stronger, more Christlike character. As teenagers learn to interpret and evaluate their decisions in light of their relationships with God, they will discover the importance of living out their faith in everything they do.

How to Use This Book

Who Am I to God? contains eight studies about the Christian faith that will help your students better understand the fundamentals of faith and how they can relate to God.

• The study about **salvation** will share God's plan for salvation with students and will encourage them to respond to God's grace in their own lives.

• The study about **faith** will help students see how having faith in God changes people's outlooks and actions.

- In the study about the **Trinity**, students will explore the relationship between Father, Son, and Holy Spirit and will seek the significance it has for their relationship to God.
- The study about the **Bible** will teach students the purpose and benefits of Scripture as well as provide some tools for understanding Scripture.
- In the study about **prayer**, students will experience prayer, evaluate their prayer lives, and think about the importance of regular prayer.
- The study about **worship** will help students understand how worship fits into their relationship with a God who is very worthy of their adoration and praise.
- The study about **sharing faith** will help students seek examples of others who have shared their faith, discover the importance of sharing their faith, and then commit to sharing their faith.
- The study about **service** will help students comprehend that service to others is not a way to gain salvation, but is actually a way of expressing our love to God.

The *Christian Character Development Series* encourages students to examine their own character in a very individual, personal way. Each study in this series guides students to examine the topic individually, in pairs, and in larger groups.

Each study connects the topic and the Scriptures to God-centered character development—the idea that God gives us a model of quality character in his Word, as well as a desire to know him and to become more like him.

Before each study, photocopy the entire study for each person. Each person in your group will have his or her own set of handouts to use extensively throughout each study for journaling and other writing and drawing activities. Each study begins with a section called "Read About It" and then follows with a section called "Write About It." These sections provide teenagers with "food for thought" about the topic and provide the opportunity to respond to those thoughts, right on their papers. You may choose to have your students complete these sections before your group meets, or you may decide to have students complete these sections at the beginning of your meeting time.

Other sections of the study are designed so students can work through them with a minimum of direction from you. Any direction you may need to give your students is included in the "Leaders Instructions" boxes. You're encouraged to participate and learn right along with the students—your insights will enhance students' learning.

Each study provides a combination of introspective, active, and interactive learning. Teenagers learn best by experiencing the topic they're learning about and then sharing their thoughts and reactions with others.

Christian Character Development Series: Who Am I to God? will help you guide your teenagers through the perils and pitfalls of growing up in today's culture. Use the studies in this book to work with your youth to understand what it means to have high standards of character and to learn why character is important to God.

Other Topics

Who Am I With Others?

Knowing God
Conflict
Forgiveness
Friendships
Parents and Other Authorities
Dating
Loneliness
Love

Who Am I When Nobody's Looking?

Honesty
Wisdom
Integrity
Humility
Trust
Generosity
Compassion
Faithfulness

Who Am I Inside?

Hope
Fear
Guilt
Pride
Joy
Grief
Anger
Peace

Who Am I to Judge?

Sex
Drugs and Alcohol
Peer Pressure
Moral Absolutes
Idolatry
Media and Music
Handling Stress
Making Good Decisions

Who Am I...Really?

Righteousness
Popularity
Success
Self-Esteem
The Family of God
Spiritual Gifts
Role Models and Heroes
Dreams of the Future

Before and After

God's saving grace reshapes our identities so that we want to love and obey God.

Supplies: You'll need Bibles, pens or pencils, and markers or colored pencils.

Preparation: Set out the supplies on a table to use during the study.

Leader Instructions

Begin by having students each read the "Read About It" section and respond in the "Write About It" section.

Read About It

Many Christian musicians use the names of their bands to express something they believe about their identity as Christians. Think about the names these groups have chosen and what the names say about Christians or Christianity:

- Point of Grace
- Watermark
- Newsboys
- Burlap to Cashmere
- Jars of Clay
- Out of Eden
- Seven Day Jesus
- Anointed

Write About It

- Which of these band names comes closest to expressing your thoughts on what it means to be a Christian?

- If you were creating a name for your own Christian band, what name would you choose? How would this name tell others what you believe about salvation?

- On a scale of one to ten (ten is high), how significant is your salvation in shaping who you are? Why did you choose that ranking?

- At what ranking would you like to be? Why? What would be different about your life at that ranking?

- In what ways might responding to God's grace change the person who responds?

Experience It

Leader Instructions

Have students form groups of three, and point out the supply table you've prepared before the study.

In your group, follow the instructions on the page titled "The ABCs of Salvation" (p. 9).

The ABCs of Salvation

Imagine that TV station CTV has called you. It's doing a special on Christianity in America and wants teenagers to explain just what the Bible teaches about salvation. Peter Lemmings is flying out to interview—of all people—you! Fortunately, Mr. Lemmings has sent a copy of the interview questions and suggested, oh so politely, that you might be more comfortable on nationwide TV if you wrote your responses in advance.

With your group, complete the following exercises to prepare for the interview:

1. Read each Bible passage listed below.
2. Share what each verse means to you. In other words, have you seen this truth in action in your own life, or how has the truth in the passage affected you?

- John 3:16
- Romans 3:22-24
- Romans 5:8
- Romans 6:23
- Romans 10:9-10

Now as a group, discuss the following interview questions, using your life experiences and the Bible passages to form your answers. Write your answers below.

Peter Lemmings: Christians talk about salvation quite a bit. In terms of market share, how large a percentage of the population would you say needs salvation, and why?

You:____

____

PL: Sin seems to be an outdated concept these days. I'm not sure our viewers understand what it is. Could you define "sin" and give some examples?

You:____

____

Tell Me More...

A few thoughts on what the Bible says about sin:

Sin is an act against God.

"Against you, you only, have I sinned and done what is evil in your sight, so that you are proved right when you speak and justified when you judge" (Psalm 51:4).

Sin is an act of breaking the law (whether God's law or man's law).

"Everyone who sins breaks the law; in fact, sin is lawlessness" (1 John 3:4).

Sin is not always an act. It might be not acting as God intends.

"Anyone, then, who knows the good he ought to do and doesn't do it, sins" (James 4:17).

PL: Let's get back to salvation. Why do we have to talk about something negative like sin to understand salvation?

You:____

PL: When you talk about sin, you're talking not only about actions that could have serious consequences, but also about actions that some people might really enjoy. Why would people want to be "saved" from those sins? And does being "saved" mean that people no longer have to face consequences for their actions? Please explain.

You:____

PL: All this talk about sin is pretty grim. Does your God offer any solution?

You:____

PL: And what do people have to do to get salvation? How does it work?

You:____

PL: Why would God do this?

You:____

PL: Now, some people think the concept of salvation is a hoax or, at best, no big deal. What's your response?

You:____

PL: Finally, how has salvation affected you? Has it made any difference in your everyday life? Please explain.

You:____

PL: Thanks for joining us. That's the good news for tonight. This is Peter Lemmings.

Leader Instructions

After groups have finished "The ABCs of Salvation," have one person play the part of Peter Lemmings and ask the interview questions. Have someone from each group respond to each question. Compare responses with questions like:

- *What differences or similarities did you notice in how groups answered?*
- *How easy or difficult was it for you to express the good news of salvation in everyday language? Explain.*
- *If you had been listening to a broadcast of this interview, what do you think would have made the biggest impression on you? Explain.*
- *What insights about God did you gain from this experience?*
- *What are some appropriate responses to God's gift of salvation?*

Tell Me More...

Romans Road

The passages from Romans that are listed in "The ABCs of Salvation" are often called the "Romans Road" because they take us step by step along the path to salvation. They also show how God works to transform a person's character as he changes those who "fall short" (Romans 3:23) into those who submit to Christ's lordship (Romans 10:9).

Apply It

Stay in your groups to complete this activity.

You've probably seen "before and after" ads for hair-growth products or weight-loss plans. Most of them aren't very believable, but God offers a before-and-after plan with an eternal lifetime guarantee.

Read each of the following passages. After each, discuss these questions:

- What word picture does this passage use for before God works in someone's life?
- What word picture does this passage use for after God has worked in someone's life?

The passages

- Galatians 3:23, 26
- Ephesians 2:1-5
- Ephesians 2:12-13, 19
- 1 John 1:5-7

Extension Idea

You may want to videotape the group interview. You can produce a simple video segment by simply filming the interview, or you may make a more elaborate production with props and setting. If you like, you may use the videotape when you discuss sharing faith in the lesson titled "A Faith Worth Sharing."

On your own, choose the before-and-after contrast that is most meaningful to you. Using that contrast, sketch your own version of yourself before and after

God's work in your life. You can add color with markers or colored pencils.

Tell Me More...

Although the before-and-after contrasts offer vivid pictures of the difference between life with and without Christ, not all believers can identify the point at which they changed from a "before" to an "after." While some Christians have experienced a radical change in their lives as a result of conversion, others may not remember a time when they didn't trust and love the Lord. What's important is not pinpointing the time of change, but knowing that your identity is that of someone who belongs to and is committed to Christ.

Share your illustrations with your group, and discuss the following questions:

- How does this before-and-after imagery influence your understanding of who you are?
- What kind of character traits would you expect an "after" person to have? Why?
- What kinds of concrete actions might those character traits translate into? Be specific.
- How can you respond this week to what God has done for you? For example, if you have received God's gift of salvation, in what specific situation can you demonstrate that you are an "after" person this week? If you aren't sure about God's salvation in your life, what do you want to do in response to what you've learned about salvation—for example, read more about it and talk with someone about it. In your group, identify a specific action or attitude each person wants to demonstrate this week, and pray for one another to follow through.

Live It

Just being able to express the ABCs of salvation isn't enough; you have to accept the good news for yourself. Spend some time this week reflecting on the following passages from the book of Romans. Read the verses, then mark an X where you see yourself on the "Romans Road."

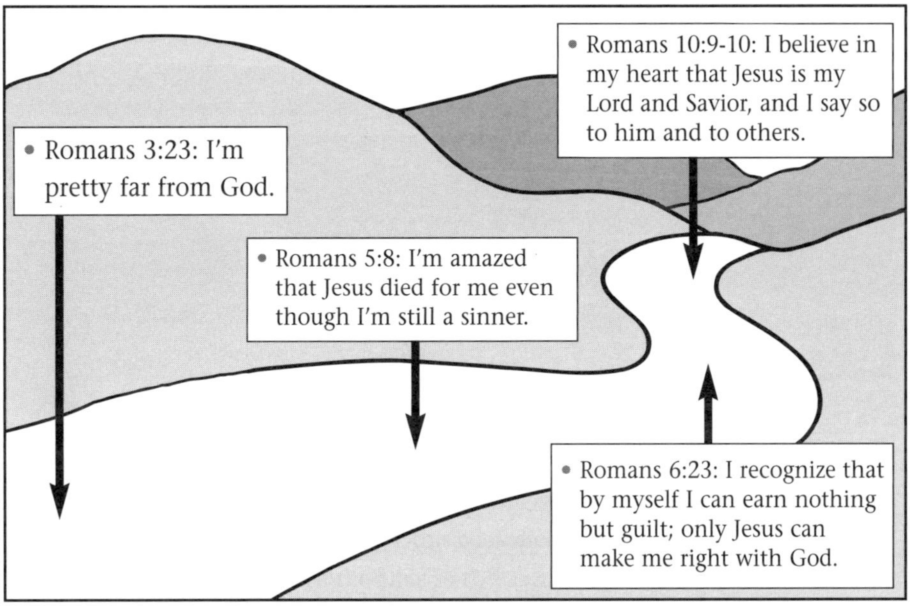

• Do you think other people would say your character reflects where you are on the road? Explain.

• If you're not where you want to be on the road, who could you talk to this week? Find that person and share your concerns.

Remember, calling on God and being saved (Romans 10:13) is not the end of the road! It's just the beginning of a thrilling, lifelong journey. If you haven't already started on that journey, you can begin right now. Sincerely pray this prayer or one of your own like it, and you *will* be saved. You have God's word on it.

Dear God,

I don't like to think of myself as a sinner, but I know I am. I disobey you in the wrong things I do, and I fall short by not doing the right things I should do. I am sorry. But on my own, I can't put things right with you. Please forgive me through Jesus Christ, who died for me and rose again. And please help me to live for you, not for myself.

In Jesus' name, amen.

Living by Faith

Faith is being sure of what we hope for.

Supplies: You'll need Bibles, pens or pencils, candles with drip catchers, and matches.

Preparation: Set out the supplies on a table to use during the study.

Leader Instructions

Begin by having students each read the "Read About It" section and respond in the "Write About It" section.

Read About It

A *martyr* is someone who is persecuted or even killed for what he or she believes. There have been many Christian martyrs tortured, imprisoned, and put to death for their faith in Christ. These people are willing to die because they are sure of what they believe.

One young pastor in Zimbabwe, Africa, was killed because of his faith in Jesus. After his death, a note was found in his office in which he declared his determination to share the message of Christ no matter what opposition faced him. A portion of the note read, "I am a disciple of Jesus. I must go till he comes, give till I drop, preach till all know, and work till he stops me. And when he comes for his own, he will have no problem recognizing me...my banner will be clear!"

(from *The Signature of Jesus* by Brennan Manning)

Write About It

- What's your reaction to this quote?

• What does the quote say about the pastor's faith?

• What do you think the pastor's banner said? What does your banner say?

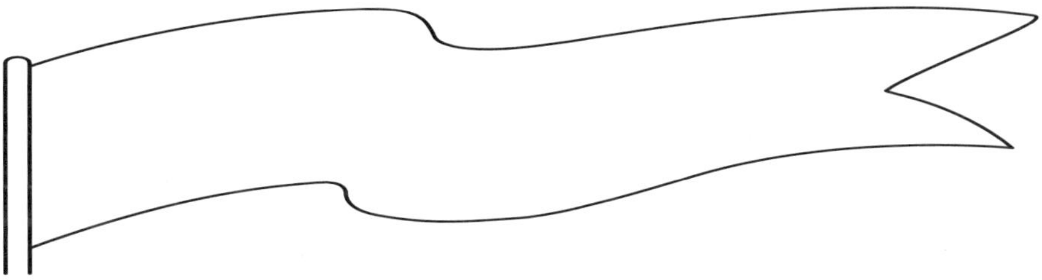

• How did the pastor reveal his banner to others? How do you reveal your banner to others?

• Read Hebrews 11:1. How does the quote illustrate a life lived with this verse in mind? How do you think an understanding of that kind of faith would affect the way a person lived?

Experience It

Leader Instructions

Have students form pairs, and point out the supply table you've prepared before the study. For the first section of the "By Faith" page, have everyone get a candle and light it. When everyone is ready, turn out the lights. When pairs have finished the first section, turn the lights back on.

Follow the instructions on the "By Faith" page (p. 16) with your partner.

Use the supplies on the supply table as needed.

By Faith

Section 1

Get a candle from the supply table and light it. When your leader turns off the lights, follow these directions:

Read Hebrews 11:8-16 together. Then discuss the questions and write or draw your answers.

- Write five to eight words from this passage that capture its most important message.
- How does the definition of faith in Hebrews 11:1 apply to Abraham?
- Why do you think Abraham had faith?
- Compare living with faith to completing these exercises by candlelight.

Blow out your candles, and wait for your leader to turn the lights back on before you begin the next section.

Section 2

Read Hebrews 11:17-19, 24-28. Then fill in the chart, and answer the questions below.

	Abraham	Moses
What they *could* see:		
What they *couldn't* see:		
What they hoped for/what God had promised them:		
What actions they took:		

- How does the definition of faith in Hebrews 11:1 apply to Abraham and Moses?
- What did these difficult situations seem to do for the faith of Abraham and Moses?
- Why do you think Abraham and Moses had faith?

Section 3

Stand up with your back to your partner, and one of you close your eyes. Now, the partner with closed eyes, gently fall backward, and let your partner catch you. After you've each had a turn, discuss these questions and write your responses:

- What was it like to do this exercise?

- How was this exercise similar to having faith in God as described in Hebrews 11:1?

- Why is it difficult sometimes to have faith?

Read 1 Peter 1:3-9, then fill in the chart below.

You

What you can see:

What you can't see:

What you hope for and what God promises you:

- What do difficult situations do for your faith?

- Why might God like you to have faith?

- What situations might you face in which having faith would be helpful?

Leader Instructions

After everyone has finished the "By Faith" pages, process the experience with the whole group by asking questions such as these:

- *What did you learn about faith from these experiences?*
- *What did you learn about your own faith?*
- *What did you learn about God? about his promises?*

Tell Me More...

Though no one is certain who wrote the epistle to the Hebrews, the author produced a very polished, structured appeal to a group of Christians who were apparently suffering persecution. Most likely writing to a group of Jewish-Christian believers, the author implores them to hold on with the faith of their forefathers and persevere in the hope they have in Christ. The author encourages the people to see beyond their current situation and reminds them that God has always been faithful and can be trusted.

Apply It

Complete these exercises with the same partner.

First think of some specific challenges in your own life. In the chart below, write these challenges in the appropriate spaces.

Extension Idea

As your students begin to work on the "By Faith" page, distribute Blow Pops or Tootsie Pops. When both partners have reached the center of the candy, have them compare eating the suckers to living with faith.

Then, for each challenge in the chart, describe only what you're able to see *without* faith. For example, if you're having a challenge with a teacher over the theory of evolution, perhaps you can see only your teacher's stubbornness.

Then—remembering God's promises, the work God has already done in your life, and the work God did in the lives of the faithful Hebrews you've read about—describe in the chart what God can help you to see *with* faith. How can God transform each challenging situation beyond what you can currently see? For example, perhaps with faith God can help you to see how your challenge with your teacher will strengthen your own faith and give you an opportunity to tell others about Jesus.

Challenge	Seeing Without Faith	Seeing With Faith
Argument over evolution with Mrs. Bradley	She's stubborn!	As I look for answers, my own faith will grow, and I may be able to tell others about Jesus.

Discuss these questions with your partner, and write your answers:

- After filling in the chart, how do you feel about your challenges?

- What can help you to view challenges *with* faith?

Now read Hebrews 12:1-3 with your partner. Use the cross below to reflect on your own faith.

MY FAITH HEROES

WHAT KEEPS ME FROM HAVING FAITH

AREAS OF LIFE IN WHICH I NEED MORE FAITH

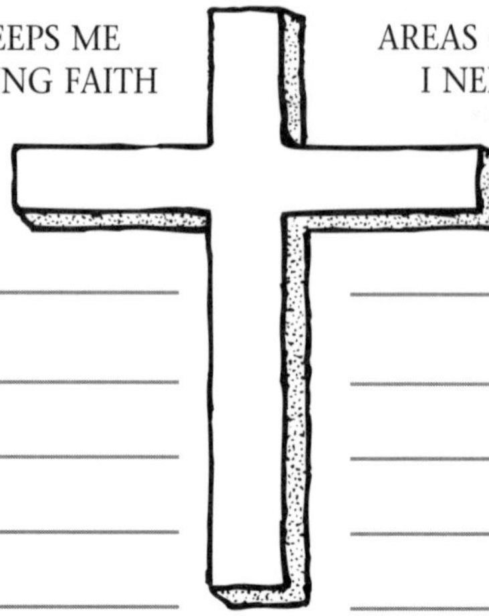

GOD'S PROMISES TO ME

Trade books with your partner. Look at your partner's cross, and then write a prayer for your partner in his or her book. Does your partner need to trust God more? need to seek help from faith heroes? need to study God's promises?

Dear God... ______________________________

Pray the prayer aloud for your partner, and then return his or her book.

Tell Me More...

"In the last analysis, faith is not the sum of our beliefs or a way of speaking or a way of thinking; it is a way of living and can be articulated adequately only in a living practice."

—Brennan Manning, *The Signature of Jesus*

Live It

Read Matthew 16:13-19.

In this passage, Jesus asks Peter a stunning faith question. It is a question that we each need to answer for ourselves. Take a poll of people you care about, asking them, "Who do you say Jesus is?" Write their names and responses on the banners on the next page. Then write your own name and response. You may also want to ask these questions:

- What choices have you made because of who Jesus is?
- What difference has your opinion about Jesus made in your life?

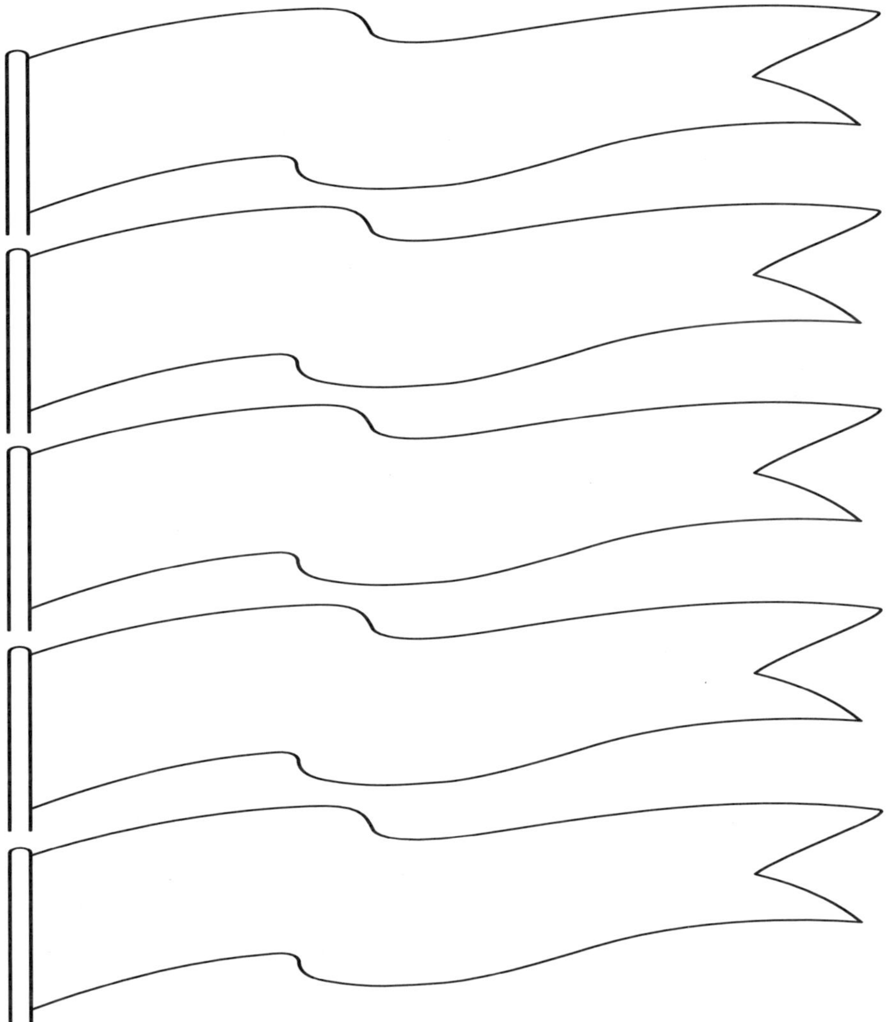

Tell Me More...

"[The people of faith named in Hebrews] all made their share of mistakes and engaged in episodes of disobedience and rebellion. But God stuck with them so consistently and surely that they learned how to stick with God."

—Eugene Peterson, *A Long Obedience in the Same Direction*

Three Are One

God reveals himself to us as Father, Son, and Holy Spirit.

Supplies: You'll need Bibles, pens or pencils, apples, napkins, and a small reading lamp.

Preparation: Set out the supplies on a table to use during the study.

Leader Instructions

Begin by having students each read the "Read About It" section and respond in the "Write About It" section.

Read About It

God has an amazing way of teaching us about himself. For example, at the very base of God's creation, we've discovered these subatomic particles called "quarks." Each proton or neutron in an atom's nucleus is a composite of three quarks. Yep, three quarks—every time. We only find them in threes, and they have never been found alone. There they are. Three in one and holding the entire world together.

The Christian church developed a concept called the Trinity to help us all understand Scripture. Though the word "Trinity" isn't mentioned in Scripture, the Bible—especially the New Testament—describes three different pictures of God: Father, Son, and Holy Spirit. These three are connected and related, they constitute one God, and they each do different things. There they are. Three in one and holding the entire universe together.

Write About It

- What's your reaction to the information about quarks? What does it tell you about God?

- How has the Trinity been explained to you before?

- If you wanted to explain the Trinity to someone else, what would you say? How might using quarks help you?

- Why do you think some people have difficulty believing in the triune nature of God?

- Why might it be important for people to understand the triune nature of God?

Experience It

Leader Instructions

Have the students form groups of no more than four, and point out the supply table you've prepared before the study. Turn on the lamp. When all the groups are ready for Section 2 of the "Triune Nature" page, have them gather around the lamp.

In your group, follow the instructions on the "Triune Nature" page (p. 24). Use the supplies on the supply table as needed.

Triune Nature

Section 1

Discuss your response to each of the following exercises with your group members.

Hold an apple in your hand. Spend a minute in silence, looking at your apple. Draw it here.

To your drawing, add the three main parts that constitute the apple you're holding: the peel, the flesh, and the core.

Remove some of the apple peel. On your drawing, write what the peel does for the apple.

Now eat some of the apple's flesh. On your drawing, write what the flesh does for the apple.

Now eat your apple till you get to the core. On your drawing, write what the apple core does for the apple.

Draw another apple here; again include the apple's three main parts.

Read Deuteronomy 4:35 and Matthew 28:19. What do these Scriptures say about God's nature? On the apple, write how it can be a metaphor to describe God's nature.

Read 1 Corinthians 8:6 and Ephesians 4:6. What do these Scriptures say about God? On the apple core, write how it can be a metaphor to describe God the Father. How is the apple core's function similar to God the Father's?

Read John 1:1-4,14 and Colossians 1:15-20. What do these Scriptures say about God? On the apple's flesh, write how it can be a metaphor to describe Jesus the Son. How is the flesh's function similar to Jesus'?

Read John 14:25-26 and Galatians 4:6. What do these Scriptures say about God? On the apple peel, write how it can be a metaphor to describe the Holy Spirit. How is the apple peel's function similar to the Holy Spirit's?

Below write what this picture of the Trinity adds to your understanding of God.

In another group member's book, write one thing you want him or her to remember about the Trinity.

Section 2

When your leader instructs you to, gather around the small lamp. Complete the following instructions, discuss the questions in your group, and write your answers below.

Read Romans 5:1-5 and 2 Corinthians 13:14.

- What do these Scriptures say about God? about the relationship between the Father, Son, and Holy Spirit?

Look at the lamp's light.

- What is the source of the light? How is that source like God the Father?

- How is the light like Jesus the Son?

- How is the light related to its source? How does that compare with the way Jesus is related to God the Father?

Take turns putting your hands close to the bulb so you can feel the heat.

- How is the heat like the Holy Spirit?

- How is the heat related to its source? to the light? How does that compare with the way the Holy Spirit is related to God the Father? Jesus the Son?

- What does this metaphor for the Trinity add to your understanding of God?

In another group member's book, write one thing you want him or her to remember about the Trinity.

Leader Instructions

After groups have completed the "Triune Nature" page, process the experience with questions like these:

- *What did these experiences teach you about the Trinity?*
- *How do you think your relationship with God could be affected by better understanding the different ways God has revealed himself to us?*

Tell Me More...

If we looked at only one human and tried to understand everything possible for humanity, we would fall short. After all, one person can't demonstrate all the emotions, talents, knowledge, and abilities of all humanity. Looking to only one person for our understanding of humanity would leave us with many misunderstandings about who humans are and the potential they have.

It's the same with God. We can understand more of who God is through his triune nature. When we turn away from an understanding of the Trinity, we leave ourselves open to misunderstandings about who God is and what God can do.

who God is

Apply It

Choose a partner from within your group. Discuss the following, and write your responses in the book.

Tell your partner about a time a friend misunderstood you.

- How did the misunderstanding affect your friend's view of you?

- How did the misunderstanding affect your relationship with your friend?

- How might misunderstanding God's true nature affect our relationship with him?

In the space below, draw a metaphor for the Trinity—perhaps from those you've explored during this lesson—that most helps you understand God.

On your drawing, write one way you could try to better understand what each person of the Trinity is like.

Now, for each person of the Trinity, write at least one word that describes what that person is like to you—"comforter" for God the Father, for example.

Finally write at least one way you could try to reflect to others the character of each person of the Trinity—"help people who are feeling down," for example.

Close by praying together that your relationship with God will become stronger as you learn about his triune nature and strive to reflect that nature to others.

Extension Idea

Use this opportunity to look at the unity and diversity of the church. Together read 1 Corinthians 12, and discuss the following questions.

- *How is this passage a reflection of the Trinity among Christians?*
- *What are some specific attitudes and actions through which Christians can reflect the unity of the Trinity?*

Tell Me More...

Many analogies have been used to help us grasp the concept of the Trinity. No analogy is perfect, but many of them do help us better understand this mystery. One author uses the analogy of prayer: "We know that it is God the Spirit who prompts us to pray and gives us motivation. We know our prayers are heard, because they are offered in the name of Jesus who intercedes for us, and we count upon the Father to hear and answer our prayers."

(from *The Gift of the Gospel* by H. Gerald Knoche)

Extension Idea

Explore relationships using the Trinity as your guide. Have partners apply the Trinitarian relationship to their own by completing the following sentences for each other:

- *One thing the Trinity teaches me about my own relationships is…*
- *One gift God has given you that will help you in your relationships is…*
- *I know that God cares about our relationships because…*
- *When I think of you, I will be praying for…*

Live It

During the week, complete the following observation journal. Whenever you glimpse anything that the Trinity helps you understand, write when and where you saw it.

- Look for signs that there is one God of the universe. These signs are a reflection of the Trinity.

- Look for things that are made of different parts, but are still one. These things are a reflection of the Trinity.

- List relationships in which you see people who are united even though they have different abilities or gifts. These relationships are a reflection of the Trinity.

Tell Me More...

Several modern-day Christian theologians have found a new way of presenting the Trinity: as a relationship. After all, God—Father, Son, and Spirit—*is* a relationship. We have always had in the Trinity a perfect example of what it means to live in community and of what God actually has in mind for our relationships with one another. For example, in her book *Amazing Grace,* Kathleen Norris says, "For Christians, the Trinity is the primary symbol of a community that holds together by containing diversity within itself."

Reading With Your Ears

We can hear God through his Word.

Supplies: You'll need Bibles and pens or pencils.

Preparation: Set out the supplies on a table to use during the study.

Leader Instructions

Begin by having students each read the "Read About It" section and respond in the "Write About It" section.

Read About It

The Bible may be the most controversial book in history. Some of those who were inspired by God to write this book died for their beliefs. In the 1500s William Tyndale translated the Bible so the common person could read it, and he was burned at the stake for his crime. Some of his followers were also burned, along with their Bibles. Today the Bible is still banned in many countries, and those who are found with Bibles are imprisoned, tortured, and put to death. Even in the United States there have been efforts to ban Bibles from schools and public libraries. Yet God's Word remains.

On this topic, the *Inspirational Study Bible* says, "The Bible's durability is not found on earth; it is found in heaven. For the millions who have tested its claims and claimed its promises there is but one answer—the Bible is God's book and God's voice."

Write About It

- If you were walking down the street and someone stuck a microphone in your face and said, "The Bible—what do you think?" what would you say?

• What do you think of the assessment of the Bible in the quote above?

• What have you heard other people say about the Bible?

• How do you think the Bible compares to any other book?

• Read Isaiah 40:8. What do the verse and the quote say to you about the power of Scripture?

Experience It

Leader Instructions

Have students form groups of no more than four. Have groups work through each section of the "Place to Hear God" page (p. 31). After each section, have everyone process the experience together using the following questions:

- *What did you discover about the Bible from this experience?*
- *Why is Scripture so important for Christians?*
- *What does this experience help you understand about the power of Scripture?*
- *What do you want to learn about the Bible?*

A Place to Hear God

Section 1

Have someone in your group choose a number between one and one thousand. The rest of the group members should try to guess the number and may not receive any guidance until they've guessed at least ten times. Someone else in the group should keep track of how many guesses it takes to get it right.

When your group has correctly guessed the number, discuss the following questions and write your answers:

- What helped you decide which number to guess? How effective was your method?

- What methods do you and your friends use to make decisions in your lives?

- How effective are those methods? What are some positive results and some negative results of using those methods?

- Think of people you know who use Scripture to help them make decisions. How effective is their method? What are some positive results or some negative results of using that method?

- When have you been able to use the Bible to help you make decisions?

Read 2 Timothy 3:16-17 and Hebrews 4:12.

- According to these passages, what is the Bible for?

- How does the Bible guide those who read it?

When you've finished this section, join the large group.

Section 2

Get back with your small group, and think of several things you would really like for people to know about you, things that would help someone know you well—"I want to be a teacher," "I am nothing like my older sister," or "I'm almost always the leader in sports," for example. Write those things in the first two pages of the following "book." When everyone has finished, pass your books around and read everyone's "story."

Discuss these questions, and write your answers in the last page of the book to the right:

- How was this exercise similar to the way God speaks to us in his Word?
- What kinds of things can you learn about God in his Book?

Read 2 Peter 1:16-21.

- Why do you think God helped men speak his Word through the Spirit?

- What's your opinion of God's Word after reading this passage?

When you've finished this section, join the large group.

God uses his Word to tell us...

Apply It

Find a partner, and discuss the following questions. Write your answers in the provided space.

- What disciplines are a part of your life? How did you incorporate those disciplines into your life?

- What relationships do you make time for in your life? How are you able to nurture those relationships?

- How is reading the Bible both a discipline and a relationship?

- How can you apply the same methods you use to work on other disciplines and relationships to Bible reading?

Make a commitment to apply at least two of those methods to Bible reading this week. To help, fill out the form below and discuss your plan with your partner. When you've developed your plan, sign your commitment and have your partner sign, too.

1. What book will you read? (Hint: The Apostle Paul's letters in the New Testament are often a good place to start.) ______

2. When will you read? ______

3. How much will you read? (Hint: You may find it helpful to begin reading a chunk of ten to twelve verses.) ______

4. What two methods will you use to help you reach your Bible-reading goal?

____

____

Your signature: ______________________________

Your partner's signature: _____________________

Close by praying for each other, asking God to help you with your commitments and to teach you about himself through his Word.

Tell Me More...

After you've read a section of Scripture, ask yourself the following questions to help process what you've read:

- What can I find in this passage to be thankful for—whether it's something I have or something I am?
- What does this passage cause me to regret? How is my life somehow different from what God has in mind for me?
- What do I want to pray about as a result of this passage?
- How do I want to respond to this passage?

Extension Idea

During the lesson, have students interview each other with the "Live It" questions and discuss their answers. You could also ask students to bring to the following session the answers to their interviews so everyone could discuss the responses.

Live It

To help you find answers to the kinds of questions people have about the Bible, interview Christians and friends with the following questions. You may want to talk to your youth minister or pastor about some books that can help you learn more about the Bible, too.

How can you respond when people say...

- the Bible isn't real?
- the Bible is full of mistakes, so why believe any of it?
- the Bible was written by people and not by God?
- the Bible just outlines the rules for Christianity like the Koran does for Islam?
- they don't care what the Bible says because they know what they believe?

I Pray Because...

Prayer connects us to God.

Supplies: You'll need Bibles, pens or pencils, markers, and sheets of poster board.

Preparation: Set out the supplies on a table to use during the study.

Leader Instructions

Begin by having students each read the "Read About It" section and respond in the "Write About It" section.

Read About It

Prayer is talking to God.

Prayer is listening to God.

Prayer is how I ask for God's forgiveness.

Prayer is how I express my loyalty to God.

Prayer is how I share my innermost thoughts with God.

Prayer is how I come into God's presence.

Prayer is worship.

Write About It

- Which of those statements about prayer best tells why you pray? How and why?

• Which of the statements teaches you something new about prayer?

Now complete your own prayer statements:

• Prayer is...

• I pray because...

• Prayer does...

• I pray the way I pray because...

Experience It

Leader Instructions

Have students form groups of four, and point out the supply table you've prepared before the study.

In your group, follow the instructions on the "Prayer Experiences" page (p. 37). Use the supplies on the supply table as needed.

Prayer Experiences

Section 1

Read Matthew 7:7-11. As a group, discuss the following questions and write in the space provided what you discuss.

- What word or phrase in this passage best gives you insight about prayer?

____

____

- How are your typical prayers like or unlike the way Jesus encourages us to pray in this passage?

____

____

- According to this passage, why do we pray?

____

____

Using a sheet of poster board and markers, work with your group to create a poster that illustrates what Jesus teaches about prayer in this passage. Be sure to keep in mind not only your own responses to the discussion questions, but also everyone else's responses.

Section 2

Think about your own prayer life. When, where, and how do you usually pray, and who or what do you find yourself praying for? Write your answers and your fellow group members' answers in the prayer chart.

	Your name	Group member's name	Group member's name	Group member's name
When I usually pray:				
Where I usually pray:				
How I usually pray:				
Who or what I usually pray for:				

Read Ephesians 6:18 together.

• What word or phrase in this verse best gives you insight about prayer?

• How does your prayer chart compare to this verse?

• According to this passage, why do we pray?

Now use the prayer chart to take turns praying for someone else in your group. Choose one thing from the person's usual prayer requests to pray about.

When you've finished praying for one another, add to your prayer poster to illustrate what you've learned about prayer from this section.

Section 3

Choose a person in your group to slowly and calmly lead the group through the following breath prayer. Group members, except for the leader, should put down anything in their hands, sit back, relax, and close their eyes. The group leader should slowly read aloud the following:

Mentally put away everything you've got to do and everything you're concerned about. Try to clear your mind and keep it empty.

Now slowly focus your attention on your breathing. Feel yourself breathing in and out. Take slower, deeper breaths. (Pause for a few breaths.)

Now allow yourself to think about God. In your mind, begin slowly repeating the name for God that you like best. With each breath you take in and out, repeat the name for God. (Pause for a few breaths.)

Now in your mind, allow a question to surface—something you need from God. Is it peace? Is it strength? Is it to live your faith? Now as you breathe, repeat that need along with the name for God. Pray as you breathe. (Pause for a few breaths.) Keep repeating your prayer as you breathe. (Pause for about two minutes of breath prayer.) Amen.

Now, together as a group, read 1 Thessalonians 5:16-18. Discuss the following questions, and write in the space provided what you discuss:

• How were you feeling during the breath prayer?

• What do this passage and this experience tell you about prayer?

• According to this passage, why do we pray?

With your group members, discuss what this passage and this experience add to your picture of prayer, and then illustrate what you've learned about prayer on your prayer poster.

Tell Me More...

"Breath prayer" is an attempt to "pray without ceasing" and has been used in the Christian church for centuries. The idea for breath prayers came from Psalms, where short phrases are often repeated throughout a psalm. One breath prayer, which has been used since the sixth century, is called the Jesus Prayer: "Lord Jesus Christ, Son of God, have mercy on me, a sinner."

Breath prayers are simple prayers that can be spoken in just one breath, that address God in a personal way, and that ask God to do something in us or to us. The idea is to let the prayer become such a part of your breathing that it becomes a part of you—thus, you pray without ceasing.

Extension Idea

Display the prayer posters so the rest of your church can see what you've experienced in prayer. You might want to add an explanation to each poster so people can understand what the posters reflect.

Leader Instructions

After the groups have finished the "Prayer Experiences" page, have the members of each group share their prayer poster and describe what they've learned about prayer. Ask questions such as these:

- *What did you learn or relearn about prayer?*
- *What did these exercises teach you about God? about yourself?*
- *How will your prayer life be affected by what you've learned?*

Apply It

Leader Instructions

Have each person take his or her book, a pen or pencil, and a Bible and find a comfortable, quiet place to be alone for this portion of the lesson.

Allow yourself to enjoy this time of quiet. Read about Jesus' prayer life in Mark 1:35.

- Why is quiet and solitude so important for prayer?

____

____

- How has God communicated to you through prayer?

____

____

• Describe what prayer does for you.

____

____

____

Extension Idea

Many churches have prayer chains, but many don't include children or youth. Begin a prayer chain with the youth, or add the youth to the church's prayer chain.

If you find it difficult to find time to pray, remember that prayer is about opening yourself to God. When and where can you do that? Use the clocks below to help you set aside some time to be with God.

"THE BEST TIME FOR ME TO PRAY EACH DAY"

"THE LENGTH OF TIME THAT I WILL PRAY EACH DAY."

Close by praying that God will help you keep this commitment and will give you this opportunity to grow closer to him.

Live It

Take these prayer starters home with you, and try to pray your way through each within the week.

- Lord, I wonder...
- Jesus, I am asking...
- Savior, because you...
- God, I thank you...
- Savior, give us...
- God, you've done...
- God, you know I...
- Jesus, when you...
- Christ, I don't know how...
- Lord, I get overwhelmed by...
- Gracious God, once again...

Tell Me More...

"To pray is to change."
—Richard J. Foster, *Prayer: Finding the Heart's True Home*

- God, I am so glad...
- Jesus, let me be open to...
- God, if you could create this whole world...

Tell Me More...

"I have learned that prayer is not asking for what you think you want but asking to be changed in ways you can't imagine...People who are in the habit of praying...know that when a prayer is answered, it is never in a way that you expect."

—Kathleen Norris, *Amazing Grace*

You Are Worthy

Worship is our response to who God is and what God does.

Supplies: You'll need Bibles, pens or pencils, old magazines, construction paper, scissors, glue sticks, and anything else you have on hand that would be good for making collages.

Preparation: Set out the supplies on a table to use during the study.

Leader Instructions

Begin by having students each read the "Read About It" section and respond in the "Write About It" section.

Read About It

What comes to mind when you hear the word "worship"? Chances are you think of singing, praying, or maybe the church where you go to worship. And that's good. Worship is something we *do,* so it's appropriate to think of the ways and the places in which we do it.

But worship ultimately isn't about us and what we do. It's about God. He is the object of our worship.

The word "worship" actually comes from an Old English word meaning "worth-ship." Worship is our response to God's worthship. He is worthy. We respond.

Write About It

- What first comes to mind when you hear the word "worship"? List three or four words.

• Why do you think God is worthy of worship?

• How is your worship a response to God's worthship?

• What does our worship communicate to God?

Extension Idea

Most of the sections of Psalm 66 end with the word "selah." No one is quite sure what "selah" means, but most people think it is a musical term of some kind. You may want to have each group choose a song that relates to its section and sing it together after its presentation.

Experience It

Leader Instructions

Have students form four groups. Assign each group one section of the "Hands-on Worship" page (pp. 44-46), and point out the supply table you've prepared before the study.

In your group, follow the instructions for your section of the "Hands-on Worship" page (p. 44). Use the supplies on the supply table as needed.

Hands-on Worship

Section 1

Read Psalm 66:1-4. As a group, discuss the following questions and write the answers in the space provided:

- What actions does this passage associate with worship? List those verbs here.

- What attitudes do those actions reflect?

- What is the *content* of the worship described in these verses? In other words, what do the worshippers shout, sing, or say?

- According to this passage, who or what is called to worship God? In what ways could this happen? Try to think of specific examples. (Look at Psalm 19 for more ideas.)

Using the art supplies provided, work as a group to create a collage or montage that shows the diversity of ways creation reflects God's glory and demonstrates his awesomeness. Put all group members' books together and create your collage or montage on all pages. This way it can be viewed as a whole but also taken apart when each person takes his or her book home.

When you've finished, discuss these questions in your group and write the answers in the space provided:

- What does your experience with this passage teach you about God's "worthship"—his worthiness to be worshipped?

- How will this impact your own experience of worship?

Section 2

Read Psalm 66:5-7. As a group, discuss the following questions and write the answers in the space provided:

- What reason does this passage give for worshipping God?

- What event does verse 6 refer to? (Check out Exodus 14 if you're not sure.) Why would this be such a significant event for God's Old Testament people?

- What other significant event(s) would you describe as a reason for worshipping God?

The Bible gives us many "snapshot" pictures of historical events—great things God has done.

Using the art supplies provided, work as a group to create a scrapbook page of "snapshots" that represents the event in verse 6 and the other event(s) you've identified as reasons for worshipping God. Put all group members' books together, and create your scrapbook on all pages. This way it can be viewed as a whole but also taken apart when each person takes his or her book home.

When you've finished, discuss these questions in your group and write the answers in the space provided:

- What does your experience with this passage teach you about God's "worthship"—his worthiness to be worshipped?

- How will this impact your own experience of worship?

Section 3

Read Psalm 66:8-15. As a group, discuss the following questions and write the answers in the space provided:

- How can testing and hard times lead to praise and worship?

- What hard times have you faced personally? How have you seen God in those hard times?

- According to verses 13 through 15, what is a worshipful response when God has brought you safely through a hard time?

- Jesus' sacrifice on the cross ended the need for the bloody sacrifices that Old Testament worshippers brought. In what ways can we respond to God today?

Using the art supplies provided, work as a group to create a collage or montage of symbols that represents the things you can offer God in response to his work in your life. Put all group members' books together, and create your collage or montage on all pages. This way it can be viewed as a whole but also taken apart when each person takes his or her book home. Some symbols may be very concrete, like a dollar to represent giving money; others may be metaphors, like a snake with a forked tongue to represent giving up gossip.

When you've finished, discuss these questions in your group and write the answers in the space provided:

- What does your experience with this passage teach you about God's "worthship"—his worthiness to be worshipped?

- How will this impact your own experience of worship?

Section 4

Read Psalm 66:16-20. As a group, discuss the following questions and write the answers in the space provided:

- According to these verses, what has God done for the writer? (Check out the verbs.) Why would that be worth telling others about?

- What has God done for you that you'd like to tell others about? How is telling others a form of worship?

- What elements of prayer do the following verses suggest? (If you know the acronym ACTS—Adoration, Confession, Thanksgiving, Supplication—see if any of these verses relate, though not necessarily in order.)
- verse 17:
- verse 18:
- verses 19-20:
- How can we offer praise in prayer when we worship privately? when we worship together?

- When we pray in worship together, what are some ways to confess our sins to God? Try to think of actions other than silently listing our sins.

- What specific requests and thanks do you have for God right now?

In your group, script a "prayer collage" that includes all of the elements from this passage. Be creative: Think of ways to involve other worshippers rather than having one person read a prayer aloud. (For example, you might invite each person in the large group to offer praise for something that starts with the same letter as his or her first name.) Then be ready to lead the other groups through your prayer.

When you've finished, discuss these questions in your group and write the answers in the space provided:

- What does your experience with this passage teach you about God's "worthship"—his worthiness to be worshipped?

- How will this impact your own experience of worship?

Leader Instructions

When all the groups have completed their sections of the "Hands-on Worship" page, have each group present its project to the other groups. Use this time to worship together.

After each group presents its project, process the experience by asking the whole group:

- *What does your experience with this section of the passage teach you about God's "worthship"—his worthiness to be worshipped?*
- *How will this impact your own experience of worship?*
- *Do you think God expects a certain kind of character from those who worship him? Explain.*
- *What character qualities could get in the way of true worship?*
- *What character qualities might the process of worship help us to develop or refine?*

Apply It

Write your own psalm, reflecting on who God is, what he does, and how you respond. Use the following sentence-starters to give structure to your psalm and to focus on concrete ways you can respond in worship this week. If you're feeling particularly creative, try setting your psalm to music—that's what King David did when he wrote psalms.

- God, when I look at your creation, I realize you are...

___

- A part of your creation that especially reminds me of your worth is...

___

- This week I want to respond to what you have done in creation by...

___

- God, when I think of what you have done in my life, I realize you are...

___

- This week I want to respond to what you have done for me by...

___

Extension Idea

For Section 1, if weather and location permit, have the group go on a scavenger hunt to find examples of how nature reflects God's glory. Group members can bring back samples, if it's ecologically sound to do so, or simply be ready to describe to the other groups what they've found.

Extension Idea

Instead of having the group for Section 2 draw the snapshots, you could provide a Polaroid camera so the group may set up shots for its scrapbook page.

Extension Idea

For Section 3, you may want to provide rocks so the third group can build an altar for its sacrifice symbols.

Live It

Worship isn't something you go to; worship is something you do. This week, take a good look at your response to God's "worthship"—his worthiness to be worshipped. Keep in mind two kinds of worship:

- Individual: Are you noticing God's worth and responding to it whenever and wherever you are?
- Communal: Are you paying attention and participating at church?

Fill in the bar graph below to reflect your level of responsiveness in each area. What aspects of worship are you good at? Where do you need to pay more attention?

This week I was				
• very responsive.				
• somewhat responsive.				
• pretty oblivious.				
	I responded to God's worth demonstrated in creation (Psalm 66:1-4).	I responded to God's worth demonstrated in his saving acts (Psalm 66:5-7).	I responded by giving an offering of thanks (Psalm 66:8-15).	I responded in prayer (Psalm 66:16-20).

Tell Me More...

"You are worthy, our Lord and God,
to receive glory and honor and power."

—Revelation 4:11a

Tell Me More...

Humility is not a sought-after character trait. Face it: Most of us would rather build ourselves up than accept a humble posture. But again and again, Scripture calls us to the posture—literally—of humility, especially when it talks about worship.

"Come, let us bow down in worship, let us kneel before the Lord our Maker; for he is our God" (Psalm 95:6-7a).

Bowing and kneeling are what servants do before masters, subjects before kings. Whenever we worship, if we truly worship, we acknowledge that God is infinitely greater than we are. He is our king; we are his subjects.

Worship calls for humility. Worship develops in us that quality. And best of all, when we achieve true humility, we discover that it's something worth achieving after all. Because humility puts us in the right position before God.

Tell Me More...

For a glimpse into worship in heaven, read Revelation 4!

A Faith Worth Sharing

We are called to share the story of God's work in our lives.

Supplies: You'll need Bibles and pens or pencils.

Preparation: Set out the supplies on a table to use during the study.

Leader Instructions

Begin by having students each read the "Read About It" section and respond in the "Write About It" section.

Read About It

"Share your toys."

"Share your candy."

"Share the playground equipment."

One of the first lessons every little kid has to learn is to share. Sometimes it's hard—when you've got something really good, why give it away? But sometimes kids discover that sharing makes things even more fun—the way sharing a ball and hoop turns solo practice into a game of one-on-one.

Why do we sometimes find it difficult to share our faith? Is it because we selfishly want to keep the good news to ourselves? Is it because we suspect no one else really wants what we have to offer? Is it that we don't know how? Or is it simply that we haven't discovered that sharing our faith makes our Christian life much more exciting?

When we learn about God's love for us and what Christ did for us, we know that the message can make a profound difference in others' lives, too. Evangelism is not about forcing someone to think the way we do; it's about helping others experience the joy of knowing God and his love.

Isn't that worth sharing?

Write About It

What keeps you from sharing your faith? Check all that apply.

- ❑ I'm not sure I really have a faith to share.
- ❑ I don't think I'd be very convincing.
- ❑ I don't know any non-Christians.
- ❑ I'd feel like a hypocrite telling others how to live.
- ❑ I'm afraid I'd lose my friends.
- ❑ I don't know the right things to say.
- ❑ I'm just plain nervous about it.
- ❑ I've had a bad experience with trying to share my faith.
- ❑ Nothing stops me; I share my faith regularly.
- ❑ Other: ____________________

- What difference might sharing your faith make for someone else's life? for your own life?

____

____

____

____

Experience It

Leader Instructions

Have students form groups of four.

In your group, read Romans 3:21-24. Do you think this is an important message for others to hear? Explain.

When your group has finished discussing the passage, work individually on the "Life Line" page (p. 51).

Life Line

How has God acted in your life? Use the space here to make a time line of your life until now. Don't include every detail of your life, but do mark significant high points, low points, and other important events, sort of like this sample.

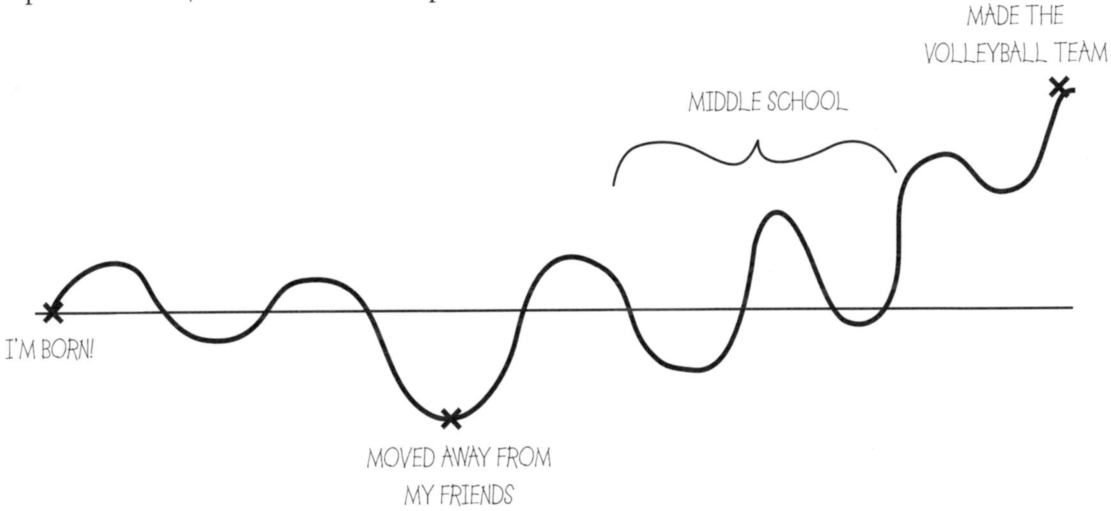

Now mark the following events on your time line (below):

- when you first learned about Jesus;
- when you personally experienced God's love (this can be in the form of another person showing God's love); and
- when you responded to God.

Share your time line with your small group. Then discuss these questions:

- How did the highs and lows affect your character? Why do you think that was the case?
- How has God affected your life? your character? Explain.

In your group, read Acts 8:30-35, discuss the following questions, and write the answers in the space provided:

- What did Philip do to share his faith?

- How, when, or where could you share your faith in the same way?

In your group, read Acts 20:35, discuss the following questions, and write the answers in the space provided:

- What did Paul do to share his faith?

- How, when, or where could you share your faith in the same way?

In your group, read Colossians 4:2-6, discuss the following questions, and write the answers in the space provided:

- What does Paul encourage us to do to share our faith?

- How, when, or where could you share your faith in that way?

In your group, read James 2:14-17, discuss the following questions, and write the answers in the space provided:

- What does this passage have to say about sharing faith?

- How, when, or where could you share your faith in that way?

In your group, read 1 Peter 3:15-16, discuss the following questions, and write the answers in the space provided:

- What does Peter encourage us to do to share our faith?

- How, when, or where could you share your faith in that way?

Extension Idea

You may want to bring in tracts that students can use to share the gospel. Most Christian bookstores have a selection of evangelistic tools. Youth for Christ produces Life's Greatest Adventure, *a booklet especially for teenagers to use in sharing their faith, and a* Life Band Witness Bracelet *that students can use with or without the booklet. (You can contact Youth for Christ at 1-800-735-3252, www.livethelife.org, or www.shopyfc.org.)*

Tell Me More...

"A lady once told an evangelist, 'I don't like your method.' He replied, 'I'm not totally satisfied with it myself. What's yours?' She answered, 'I don't have one,' to which the evangelist responded, 'I like my method better than yours.' "

—G. Michael Cocoris

Apply It

Leader Instructions

Have students form pairs.

With a partner, read Acts 1:8 and discuss the three P's in this passage:

- Power: What power did Jesus promise the disciples? How do you experience that power in your life? When do you most need that power?
- Project: What about this passage indicates that God's project of evangelism was not an option for the disciples? What role do you see yourself playing in God's project of evangelism?
- Priorities: The disciples were to start sharing their faith in Jerusalem—that's right where they were. Next on the priority list were Judea and Samaria—an expanded circle of influence around Jerusalem. Then finally the gospel would reach "to the ends of all the earth."

With your partner, think about who is closest to you. Fill in the target below with specific names.

With your partner, brainstorm practical, specific ways you could share your faith with the people in your "Jerusalem" circle. Put a check mark by the actions you will take this week.

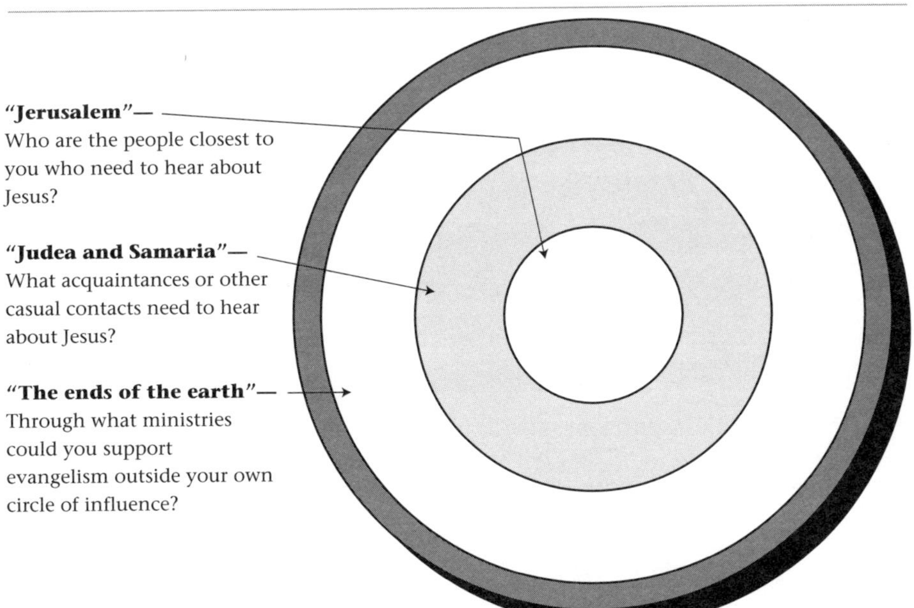

Tell Me More...

You can't share what you don't have. If you aren't sure that Jesus is your Lord and Savior, this week talk to a Christian you trust and respect.

Live It

Hold yourself accountable to the commitment you've made to share your faith this week. At the end of each day, draw in the day's box as many of the following symbols as apply:

I noticed an opportunity to share my faith today.

I created an opportunity to share my faith today.

I used an opportunity to share my faith today.

I wasted an opportunity to share my faith today.

I spent time building a relationship with someone I soon plan to share my faith with.

Day 1	Day 2	Day 3	Day 4	Day 5	Day 6	Day 7

At the end of the week, reflect on these questions:

- What was easy for you?

- What was difficult?

- Where do you need to tap into God's power to be his witness?

The Full Extent of Love

Study 8

We express our genuine love for God through service to others.

Supplies: You'll need Bibles, pens or pencils, one gift box for each person (various sizes are OK), wrapping paper, bows, tape, colored markers, and other decorative supplies.

Preparation: Set out the supplies on a table to use during the study.

Leader Instructions

Begin by having students each read the "Read About It" section and respond in the "Write About It" section.

Read About It

In 1979 a woman named Agnes Gonxha Bojaxhiu won the Nobel Peace Prize. Her name doesn't sound familiar because when she was a young woman, she changed it to Mary Teresa and was later called Mother Teresa. What did this one woman do that was so profound and that touched the hearts and lives of so many? She obeyed the words of Jesus.

In Matthew 25:35-40 Jesus said that when we feed the hungry, give water to the thirsty, welcome strangers, provide clothes for those in need, care for the sick, and visit those in prison, we are doing these actions to him. Mother Teresa took these words to heart, obeyed them, and won worldwide recognition. She said, "I see God in every human being. When I wash the leper's wounds, I feel I am nursing the Lord himself. Is it not a beautiful experience?"

Write About It

- Why do you think Mother Teresa became so famous?

- Mother Teresa showed her love for God in her actions to others. How have you seen others do this same thing?

- On a scale of one to ten (ten is high), rate your trust in God's unconditional love. Explain why you chose that rating.

- What do you think of Mother Teresa's claim that we can see God in the hurting? Other than being with the poor, how can you follow this example?

- Read 1 John 3:18-20. What's the difference between loving with words and loving with actions? Why is it important to love with actions?

Experience It

Leader Instructions

Have students form small groups, and point out the supply table you've prepared before the study.

In your group, follow the instructions on the "Sheep or Goat?" page (p. 57). Use the supplies on the supply table as needed.

Sheep or Goat?

Section 1

Read Matthew 25:31-46. As a group, discuss the following questions and write the answers in the space provided:

- In one sentence, what is the main point of this passage?
- How would you describe the sheep? the goats?
- What do you think might have motivated the sheep to serve?
- In your world, who are some of "the least of these"?

Reflect on the next few questions by yourself. When all your group members have finished, move on to Section 2.

- Put yourself in this scene. On which side of the Son of Man are you standing? Why?
- How do you feel about your position in this scene?
- If you could, would you change where you're standing? Why?

Section 2

Complete the chart by answering the following questions (list as many examples as you can), then share your answers with your group:

- For the first row: When have you done these things?
- For the second row: Who else have you seen do these things, and when? (Include group members if possible.)
- For the third row: How else could you do these things?

"I was hungry and you gave me something to eat."	"I was thirsty and you gave me something to drink."	"I was a stranger and you invited me in."	"I needed clothes and you clothed me."	"I was sick and you looked after me."	"I was in prison and you came to visit me."

Think of one thing you personally can do to serve someone in the room right now. Ask that person if you can serve him or her in this way, then do it. Once your group members have completed their acts of service, continue by discussing these questions:

- How does it feel to know that whatever you've done for "the least of these," you've done for Jesus?

- In this parable, Jesus includes six examples of how love for God can be expressed through service to others. What other examples can you think of?

As a group, create a new chart. Fill in the top categories based on your answers to the last question. Then fill in each row following the instructions above.

When all groups have completed their charts, take a few minutes to share some of your categories and examples of how you could do those things.

Section 3

Read Ephesians 2:8-10. As a group, discuss the following questions and write the answers in the space provided.

- Define the following words:

Grace

Saved

Faith

- Based on this passage, how would you respond to someone who said that you have to be good to get to heaven? In other words, how do you explain the relationship between being saved by grace and doing good works?

Each person needs to take a box from the supply table. Ephesians 2:8 says that salvation is a gift from God. Decorate your box as if it were God's gift of salvation to you. Somewhere on your box, rewrite Ephesians 2:8-10 as if God were writing directly to you. Take your box home with you, and put it somewhere in your room as a reminder of what you've learned in this study.

Section 4

As a group, think of one person you know or have heard about who demonstrates a strong relationship with God. Focusing on character traits, make a list of words that describe that person.

How does this person serve others? How much time during a week do you think he or she spends serving others?

Individually, write a letter to this person that tells why your group chose him or her and what you admire about this person. Include an action plan telling the person how you will begin to show love for God through service to others.

Share your letters with your group, and then choose one letter to read to the class.

Apply It

As a group, read John 13:1-17 and discuss the following questions:

- Reread John 13:1b. How does Jesus demonstrate the full extent of his love? How else did Jesus demonstrate his love with his life?

- How can we show we love Jesus?

- Jesus asked his disciples: "Do you understand what I have done for you?" Do you? What has he done for you?

- What reasons does this passage give for serving others?

Leader Instructions

Have students form a large circle. Everyone will need a pen and his or her book. At the appropriate times, signal the beginning and end of a minute of silence. While fun, this activity should be done in a spirit of prayer.

On the "Washing Their Feet" page (p. 61), trace and outline of all or part of your foot and write your name below it. Beginning with the person to the left of the group leader, take turns prayerfully reading one verse each from John 13:1-17. Allow for a minute of silence after reading the passage to contemplate Jesus' service to us and our service to others.

After the silence, quietly pass your book to the person on your right. Focusing on character traits, write one encouraging thing in the footprint of the person's book you now hold. For example, you could write, "I admire your sensitivity to others" or "Thank you for being so friendly when I first visited this group." If possible, focus your affirmation on ways group members have served Jesus by serving others. Keep passing books until you've written in each footprint and have received your own book back. Still in a spirit of prayer, read the encouragement written to you, imagining each positive statement as a hand lovingly washing your foot.

Washing Their Feet

Live It

Having completed this study, again rate your trust in God's unconditional love on a scale of one to ten (ten is high). Has your rating changed? Explain why you chose that rating.

Extension Idea

If your group has never had a foot-washing experience, you may want to include one. You'll need several basins of warm, soapy water, wash rags, and towels for drying. You can form a circle and allow everyone to wash the feet of the person to his or her right. Another method is to enter a time of quiet prayer, allowing teenagers to listen for direction from God as to whom they should serve in this way. Prayerfully and carefully done, a foot washing can be a powerful experience of service, healing, reconciliation, and love.

- Who are three people you consider servants?

Arrange a time to interview at least one of them this week, and ask them these questions:

- How do you serve others?
- What motivates you to serve?
- What relationship do you find between your love for God and your service to others?
- What frustrations do you find in serving others? what joys?
- What advice would you give me as I look for ways to serve others?

Do you know your spiritual gifts? According to Ephesians 4:11-13, God has given every believer a gift for the purpose of giving him glory and serving others within the church. If you haven't taken a spiritual gifts test, ask your group leader if he or she can recommend one. Also, spend some time reading about spiritual gifts in 1 Corinthians 12.

Once you know your gifts, ask around at church to see who else shares your gifts. Ask them how they use their gifts to serve others, and ask if you can tag along with them next time they serve. Record your thoughts in your journal.

Tell Me More...

"What I can do, you cannot. What you can do, I cannot. But together we can do something beautiful for God."

—Mother Teresa

Tell Me More...

"I don't know if I'm going to heaven. I'm just not that good." Probably one of the most basic struggles in Christianity is the struggle between being saved by grace and doing good works. We don't feel good enough, and we can't wrap our minds around the amazing fact of God's grace.

But the Bible is pretty clear. Consider these truths:

- Even though we could never deserve it, Jesus died for the forgiveness of our sins (John 3:16; Romans 3:23-24; and Colossians 1:13-14, 2:13).
- When we accept the gift of his grace and are therefore saved, he adopts us as his children (John 1:12-13 and Ephesians 2:8-9).
- Once he comes into our lives, Christ will never leave us (Matthew 28:20 and Hebrews 13:5).
- The life Christ gives is eternal and begins when we first meet him (John 17:3 and 1 John 5:11-13).
- We don't earn salvation. It doesn't depend on us at all. God, out of incomprehensible love for us, offered us an incredible gift—his own Son, and salvation through our faith in his Son.

So can we accept God's gift and then do whatever we want? No. In Romans 6:1-2 Paul says, "What shall we say, then? Shall we go on sinning so that grace may increase? By no means! We died to sin; how can we live in it any longer?" God created us to do good works, and once we accept the gift of salvation, we are free from sin and free to do the things God has planned for us (Ephesians 2:8-10).

Let me say it again: Christians do good things *because* of God's gift to them, *not* to earn their way to God. Trying to live the Christian life can feel constricting—like a list of rules—unless we realize that we live in God's grace all the time.

Tell Me More...

Teenagers both need and enjoy hands-on service projects. Providing opportunities for your students to serve others may be one of the most important things you do for them. And while service projects may seem to require a level of seriousness or maturity that many teenagers don't appear to possess, the very act of serving may grow kids in their relationship with God in ways you never expected.

Talk with leaders in your church about ways students can serve those in the congregation. Ask church members who are active in the community about service opportunities. Call your local rescue mission, homeless shelter, crisis pregnancy center, or thrift store to see if they'd welcome help. World Vision's *Thirty-Hour Famine* is an annual program held every February aimed at raising teenagers' awareness of the world around them and how they can make a difference. Once you start looking for them, you'll be surprised at the open doors available to people who love in God's name.